STRONGER

THAN

MY

OWN

DEMONS

STRONGER

THAN

MY

OWN

DEMONS

NIGEL SHAUN DOWNING

This is a work of fiction.

Names, characters, places and incidents originate from the writer's imagination. Any resemblance to actual persons, living or dead, is purely coincidental.

First published in 2021.

To my own mother, who has given her efforts tirelessly over all my years. Thank-you from the bottom of my heart, for teaching me self-reliance, and for showing me how to have patience in looking for the lessons learned from hard times. God bless you mum.

Acknowledgements

It would be foolhardy to try to acknowledge everyone for this book, but the ones I will give a nod to for the help I have been given must mention Helen Boutle and Hayley Youell at Creative Recovery for guiding me out of my shell. Also to a very good friend of mine Alan Brookes,who has seen me go through so much and been there for me all these years. You all know how much love I have for you.

By the same author-

LIFE IS

EXIMIUS ORDO

All proceeds from Stronger Than My Own
Demons will go to mental health charities.

CONTENTS

Most people who become depressed all too often reach a point where they think or believe that no one else around them can understand what they are experiencing. This is usually accompanied with difficulty finding words to express how they are feeling. Unfortunately, or fortunately, I know from my own experiences just how lonely and isolating suffering from depression can make you feel.

This book is my attempt at explaining myself through poetry in those dark times. Hopefully you may find words which you can relate to and hence you won't feel quite so alone-at least, that is what I hope for.

I am bipolar, and over the last 28 years I have been suicidal countless times. Fortunately for me, I have learned to recognise I am very ill, although it has never made it any easier. I hope you can see from my journey from total despair through to the rays of hope and out the other side that depression never lasts forever, no matter how strongly it feels so.

Many thanks for taking your time to read this book, and hopefully if you find something to relate to then hopefully I am there with you.

Nigel Shaun Downing.

I BELIEVE

Thank-you for the lending of time

But now I don't believe I belong-

This system is wrong.

I was born then torn,

Ripped up and worn,

Down to a shred of a man.

Now all I can do,

Is try my best to redeem,

And be the best that I can

To believe in all that I'm taught-

That here my soul belongs to Thee,

And not one part of it can be bought.

So teach me how to reach them,

In words so softly spoken,

So that my deeds can reach them,

And your word is left unbroken.

I use to fly,

But now I want to die-

This life is empty,

My beating heart's a lie.

There's no one near me,

I wish I was taken,

All is lost,

And I feel forsaken.

Token gestures is all I find,

No-one is near me-

I am left behind.

Adrift and barely afloat,

All of my life is a joke-

Everyone is laughing,

But I just want to choke.

I know a painful death,

Will leave me bereft,

Yet it's all I have got now,

There's just nothing left.

Let me go,

'cos I'm on my knees,

All of my life is a joke-

So give me death,

Please.

NO FRIEND

I have no friend,

This is the end-

I see it all in sight,

Nothing tonight,

To end this fight,

Nothing in me,

No friend to end this plight.

It's strangled by my own neck,

For way too long,

Just death and its demons,

To take me where I belong.

No fight in the night,

To put things right,

It's all done,

The devils' war is won,

So reverse my light,

And stop my sun,

Kill my heart and take me-

Into from where I begun.

NOOSE.

Desolate.

Dark.

Pain so stark.

Colossal void-

Heart destroyed.

Blood turned cold,

Bones turned old.

No sparkle to the eye,

Too dry to cry.

Ready to die.

No God for the soul-

Its already sold.

Weighted down feet-

Accepting defeat.

Life detested,

All hope arrested.

Noosed rope confessed to,

Nothing to profess to.

Soon to be gone,

Where I belong

CUP

I see myself in the silence,
As it offers me a cup,
I know the truth lies in splinters-
Now I know it's time to give up
For rashness knows no reason for pity,
Nor hope for that silent choking,
Of non-ideas on lost identity-
Strewn across a barren lake.
Causing fears of unimaginable consequences,
As one more breath I take.
In muted wonder,

I grasp myself across the abyss that surrounds
me-

And prey it's not too late,

I cast myself towards my God-

And prey He isn't fake

FACELESS

Dark days show their ways,

In the cruelest of their kind.

In the darkness chasing shadows,

On the walls of my own mind-

Monotone and monochrome,

With no pocket of light for a fight.

Dark never-ending tunnels,

The submersion from the light.

No rays of hope,

Where there is no sun,

Just darkness and its' garrote,

Waiting to be hung.

No warmth of hope,

To distil away despair,

No faith in the future,

For the faceless man-

Standing there.

VESSEL

Gone,

Empty,

Lost.

Painful past catching up-

Finally paying the cost.

Feeble,

Numb,

Weak-

Future looking bleak.

Dead,

Silent,

Dumb-

Life's embers nearly done.

Scorched by defeat,

Folding in the heat.

Seems the battle is over,

And my captors war is won-

Vacant vessel paying the cost.

In any direction,

Truly lost.

BLACK FOG

Black fog black fog leave me alone,

Why do you always find me,

When I am on my own.

Black fog black fog in the middle of the day,

Black fog you fill me with dismay,

Why cannot you be the light,

And fill me instead with delight?

Why do you have to fill me with the darkness,

And run distress?

And turn darkness into weep,

From something into nothing-

A twisting oh so deep.

Black fog black fog:

Where no-one else is there,

Black fog black fog:

Where no-one else can care.

Black fog black fog,

Why do you stand there and stare?

Black fog black fog,

Why is it you do not care?

DEATHS ENVELOPE

Use my rhyme at will,
Instead of taking insidious route of the pills,
For when pain strikes like this,
It's only slowly it kills.
Hide behind the words,
Instead of listening to the thunder of the absurd,
Let's hope it's not too late,
And I can recarve my own fate,
Instead of seemingly willing,
To walk towards the devil at his gates.

Just to avoid my paralysed spine with its
chilling,

Just to avoid my paralysed spine with its
chilling,

Wishing I could be forever entombed-

Back in my very own mother's womb.

Away from the stinging of all open wounds,
Or for else deaths envelope-

Soon.

THE DEVILS MILLS

The devil and his thrills

Cut you in his mills

And lest you forget

He'll hold you to regret

That temper easily lost

Harder to pay the cost.

Misunderstanding for lack of truth

A painful landing

For lack of proof.

No caution in the message to be sending

No lack of pain without its ending

Slack and unreighned

Your anger goes unrestrained

Ill deeds without relenting

Easing pain if there was relenting

Thoughtless with lack of heed

Bought away from the ones that bleed

Slack jaw

Yet away from the score

Wanting more all the time

Never drawing the line.

Which side would you desire

If the flames get higher and higher

The devil and his mills

Cut you for his thrills

TWISTED TENDRILS

The boring monotonous voice of despair,

The ticking of a clock,

That does not care.

The twisted tendrils of thoughts in my head,

Wishing me dead.

A dark grip that's howling,

Like the calling of wolves,

Scratching fiercely,

Slowly it drills.

No hope to hold,

Like a candle in the dark:

Just stark relentless voices,

Wishing me their ills!

The dark cloak,

That shrouds away the truth,

Hides Her deceptively,

From showing me the proof.

The rattle of the demons chains,

Causing almost unbelievable pain!

Then,

Just as the strain becomes too much:

She caresses me,

With her magic touch,

Enlightened and elated,

Surrounded by happiness,

Unabated.

Encapsulated in total pure bliss,

But how I wish,

Just for a while,

This bipolar disorder

Would give me a miss!

MY LIFE !

My life's so boring!

A hearse I wish to arrange.

Strange are the thoughts,

That enter my mind,

A jumbled up haze,

Is all that I find.

I'm dark and feeling low,

With nowhere to go-

Slow is brain,

Without elastic flow.

There's no money in the meter,

And I just don't know-

I want to talk to Peter,

And then to Gabriel-

For this I have I do not need-

I'm living in my hell!

THESE DARK THOUGHTS

These dark thoughts echo so loud,
At what's now been found,
Uncaring and chasing,
And shouting so loud.
Wishing my arms to be folded,
Six foot underground-
Yes it's dark,
But so it is in here,
The stark reality within me,
Has ripped away all my veneer.
And there's no handles to carry me,
And nothing to settle me down here on Earth,
I've done with conflict and fighting,
For at the end of it what am I worth,
So throw salt all over me,

And let me lift off this lifetimes curse

NO LIGHT

It's dark in here,

There is no light,

If I still have a heart it's heavy now-

And I can no longer fight.

All night I believe there's nothing positive,

On which to feed,

And now I need to go,

Quickly leave.

I don't care how I exit,

For nothing can cause more pain,

I cannot face one more day like this-

Too many months have been the same.

In pitch black silence of a walled in mind,

I cannot let any-one in,

For they'd be scared of what they find.

I'm too far gone,

Nothing can be won,

What would be the point,

In trying to find a start,

When I've nothing for a heart?

I'm in debt and need to pay the wages,

For my life speeding across its stages,

And leaving me early- at its end.

No friend have I to understand,

There's no leaning shoulders to bend,

Who would lend me them anyway,

When all are far away?

All too busy in happy times,

To give me the time of day.

So come what may,

I feel i must go,

Although I know nothing,

Of what comes after last moment past,

This veneer I'm showing here,

Can no longer be outward cast.

KEEP ASKING WHY?

I keep asking myself why,

My defeated heart just wants to die?

For so long now,

My feet won't march to a song,

My gaze points low,

There's nothing more to see,

Light has gone,

The darkness has come along-

I just don't know,

Where I went wrong.

I want to arrest,

The rising and falling of my chest,

I've just detested it oh so long.

Yes this heavy heart,

Wants to go back to the start,

For light no longer beams around me,

So it seems I've done everything wrong.

Non understanding friends,

Have left me to fight my own ends,

And it sends me downward in a spiralling spin,

I just don't know any longer,

How to find a fight from where to begin.

I can no longer put on a show,

So now it's time-

For me to go.

STUFF IT

It's time to snuff it,

My lungs no longer want to puff it.

What's the point in me breathing any-more,

When I have just become the demons puppet?

Yet how shall I go?

In this month long split second-

I just don't know.

I care not for the method,

I'm just sick of hearing my own blood flow.

Yet not in a way to cause others suffering,

For I know living offers no release,

Yet again who cares for me,

When I'm left to carve my own inner peace?

I'm drowning anyway so a river is fine,

Yet the pain is already so sharp,

So a blade to a bloodline,

Medications a staple station,

Freely available across the nation.

Either of these offer freedom,

From this ugly incarceration.

I could hang to choke inside a noosed rope,

But then to the one who found me,

Would no longer laugh or joke.

Not at least like the joker,

Jesting at me now,

At my struggle at exit of plight,

Where the only fight I can muster,

Is how to disappear somehow.

Yes I hear the baying jackals,

Pulling me in all directions,

And tightening up my shackles,

Delighting in my fighting of how,

To be drawing my very last breath,

Yes, come and do your merry dance with me-

For all I pray for,

Is death.

IF I AM ASKED

If I am asked,

If I want to die,

It's because everything lies-

Today, tomorrow ,

The wind and the skies,

For all those once gave hope,

In its thought, feeling and glance,

Now I feel a noosed rope,

Can only give me my last chance.

Don't set yourself a task,

And definitely do not ask,

For you cannot understand,

I'm way past caring,

For you have come too late,

For where were you back in time?

Before all this attitude isolate?

So do not now hold out your hand,

For I feel like my blood no longer runs,

My heart is faint as if it should,

My mind is desolate.

My hands are destined to be empty to hold
nothing,

Like I say,

You come way oh way too late,

I've nothing to show,

So please now go,

You cannot see or feel a sliver or streak,

My legs that hold me just to steady,

Feel ready to break,

As they are weak.

I am hollow,

Yet feel no self sorrow,

I know the true meaning,

Of future bleak.

So leave me to my fate,

For your concern,

Now you finally stop and turn-

I'm sorry now,

But you're just too late.

SPINNING

The spin of the mind,

What wanton web it weaves,

Leaving nothing untouched behind,

In the searching,

Or so it seems.

Moments caught,

Then held in suspension-

The pain of time taught,

Brought along for attention.

Incomprehension of tales,

To hang in the air,

Fluttering intently,

In open suspension-there.

Trying to flee,

From the struggle of its' kind,

Suspended in a thousand pieces-

With the want of only one to find.

GRIEF

Grief,

Like a fluttering falling leaf,

Changing with the wind,

Yet offering little relief-

One small climb,

And then fall back down,

Rest for moment,

Silent in position,

A half smile lift,

Then the mental drown.

Just a swirl in the dust clouds,

Of the bottom-

Thoughts of those no longer here,

But unlike that falling leaf-

They won't be forgotten.

SLEEPLESS

Another sleepless night-

Another endless fight,

No listful bliss-

Oh how I wish!

Endlessly counting,

In hope of the magic number,

Alive turning cogs,

Keeping me from my slumber.

Synapses firing as if at war to their death,

Soldiering on as I count every breath!

Relaxed am I in nearly every sense of the word,

But the constant chatter in my head is absurd!

Not one more word do I wish to hear,

But I haven't heard the last,

Alas I fear!

Around and around on a carousel,

This night is shaping up,

To be a night from hell.

Count sheep over a fence?

I take offence.

There's too much clatter and din.

I'd begin again and try a new tact,

For just when I think the show is over,

They put on another act.

Well this sure ain't a comedy,

But I'd be laughing with a remedy,

The tricks my mind plays on me!

Emblazoned on my brain,

A relentless one-way conversation,

From which I'm beginning to strain-

No single train of thought,

But many travelling tracks,

No ticket have I bought,

No map to get it back.

Tired and forlorn,

Weary and worn,

How I wish this voice would stammer to a halt,

And my hearts hammering to cease.

Give me a chance to answer you back,

When you give your attack,

I have only one word-

Please!

LUCIFER

Lucifer in the flesh,

Push me down and turn,

To put me to the test.

Demonic sardonic smile-

To chase me mile upon mile,

Torment unrelenting,

In all forms of its presenting,

Leaving me using up silent strength all the while.

Sitting here alone with no rest-

Pushing for who is the best,

Lucifer in the flesh.

So close all the while,

Chasing me with that smile-

Lucifer in the flesh,

Putting me to the test.

WALKING INTO THE SUN

Walking into the sun often sounds like oh so much fun:

For when you're down and beat,

And off your feet,

It just seems to all make sense, in all its' recompense,

A repose to a suppose that all will be fine.

It's in the sublime just for a chance to change,

And though it now seems strange,

It's a change I must take-but tentatively and not negative,

For this must surely be better,

Than walking into the sun.

LIGHTS OUT

Who turned the lights out? Who made it all
scream and shout?

Who made it all collide,

From every angle deep inside?

Who gave it all, all this thrust into no-one that
man can trust?

Who turned the white into total black?

Who put my own colours into one attack?

Who took my truth and turned them into lies?

Who gave me my white and turned them
through that black?

Who counted me yet forgot me in the mount:

As I fly in darkness waiting for the count.

To surmount this dark stallion I do not wish to ride,

It's reign within a lack of hope:

And to choke on its' black smoke,

Living as I breathe trying to retrieve,

A will somewhere in a want-a magic wand I must weave:

For somewhere near on choke,

For it is surely one dark ghost that forever I would not wake:

Nor would I wish to give it life, never-for my sake,

To ride these horses must be a sin, six-fold of them to one of me,

With many hooves and their clatter and din,

Take me away as fast as they arrived, their energy from black-

Time out now I have seen them, it's my life
that's under attack.

At last-they're contrived from my own mind...

..see it now as I see it clear:

I have one horse near,

My horse is white and through the darkness of
this night,

As a knight I have rode her along,

Through the fear I rein her near,

And she has won all along.

PARRY AND THRUST.

I'll stay up all night,

'til I bleed on my knees from the fight,

See I know I am right to deny you,

And faith and truth will prove the Light,

And get me through.

I hear the voices calling,

Trying to stall me,

As you crept up on me without warning.

I refuse to warm to your incessant jesting,

So invest in me all you can try.

So defy you I must.

Shield and sword I carry,

As I parry you and thrust.

It's getting dark,

And my heart beats getting faint,

But do not underestimate your fate,

I am just about to start,

But for you it's getting late-

See you carry no weight,

And your dark cloak is ragged and thin.

I see you for what you truly are,

And I'm not scared to say I will win,

So slash, cut and gash my skin-

Remember just when you think its over-

Only then will I begin.

ANGEL BY MY SIDE

I feel your presence by my side,

You are my angel, un-denied.

Keep self from harm,

And spirit warm,

You show me the direction,

When I'm far from home.

You find me words,

When I cannot speak,

Give me courage,

When the world looks bleak.

And hold me steady,

When I'm feeling weak.

Angel by my side,

You give me fortitude,

Make me stronger day by day.

Guide me through life's obstacles,
In your very own special way.
I could never take you for granted,
Or your love so pure and strong,
You walk in front and guide me,
Show the errors when I am wrong.
I know I will walk through life,
With nothing to show for proof-
But with my angel by my side,

I know we know the truth.

WHEN A TEAR

When a tear, feels oh so near,

Just look up to the sky.

When pain envelopes and you cannot cope:

Leave out the question as to why.

For a reprieve if you believe, will come back to you,

When it feels oh so real in that envelope of terror, that you find when you're on your own:

Don't try to run faster and further away:

See the lies you tell yourself,

The fear left to grow and build,

For sake of lack of coping, or so it seems and feels,

No hope is not the answer:

For today the dread must be read,

Grasped, gripped and whipped:

Into shape from an untrustworthy form,

Like a penny cast adrift for a wish,

To the water and far out to see-set it free,

The lies seen against the shimmering,

Of hope and a glint of glee:

Dark cloak removed and sent out adrift,

Despair named as the demon evil at its craft:

So plain now for all to see.

So when the darkness descends, do not fear,

Just look up to the sky...

..hold it near,

For one glimmer of light,

And the answer as to why.

CRACKS (PART 2)

There's nothing to fill the gaps,
And I'm falling through the cracks!
Sometimes intelligence in motion,
Can cause oh so much commotion.
Like a runaway train inside my brain,
With no way to slow the locomotion.
My mental peace is under attack,
Find me a way of getting it back.
The constraint and the squeeze,
Is bringing me to my knees,
Help me please if you can.
I've been here before,
And I know the score,

I need to find where all this began.

But just for now can you help me somehow?

Maybe just hold my hand and a shoulder to cry,

Help me unravel the reasons why.

Maybe it's because I try to go it alone,

Walk a lonely road,

Just to find my way home.

Maybe you could guide me to the path,

Away from the confusion of this mental wrath.

Slip your hand in mine if you'll be so kind,

Maybe between us there's something we can find.

So step with me and we'll walk along,

Find a quiet place where I belong.

For strong now I need you to be,

Part with some steel to give to me.

If you could I'd thank-you for sharing,

And be eternally grateful-

Just for caring.

WATCHING ENTRAILS

I SIT AND WATCH THE ENTRAILS OF MY
CONFUSION,

PROFUSE IN THE SPEWING OF MY
MIND,

CATCHING UP IN TIME SINCE THEY'VE
BEEN AWAY,

DISMAYED THAT ITS TENTACLES CAN
REACH ME TODAY.

THE DEMONS HAVE THEIR GRIP,

AROUND MY NECK,

CHATTERING CONSTANTLY,

ABOUT WHAT I CANT FORGET,

TRYING TO GET MY GRIP ON THE TRIP
OF MY MIND,

TRYING TO FIND A LEVEL GROUND,

OR SOMETHING OF ITS KIND.

BUT TORMENT UNRELENTING IS ALL
THE DEVIL SENT,

IN NO UNCERTAIN TERMS,

AM I SURE OF HIS INTENT-

TWISTING THE CROSSES IN THE
CHAPEL OF MY MIND,

I'M FIGHTING FROM ALL CORNERS,

TO LEAVE WITH NOTHING LEFT
BEHIND.

BURN DOWN MY ALTER IF YOU MUST,

BUT I SERVE ONLY ONE GOD,

AND IT'S HIM THAT I TRUST.

YOU CANNOT COCOON ME,

AND CHRYSALIS ME TO YOUR SIDE,

WHEN MY GOD APPEARS,

IT'S YOU WHO WILL RUN AND HIDE.

MY METTLE WILL SETTLE,

FOR NOTHING BUT THE TRUTH,

THIS MAN YOU SEE BEFORE YOU,
IS NOTHING BUT LIVING PROOF.

IN THE DARKEST DAYS

It has been in the darkest days,

That I have leaned on you,

And in the darkest hour,

You were there to pull me through.

It's true I'm grateful,

For your ever present guide,

The helping hand extended,

As we walk along side by side.

When times are tough,

You're there to care,

And remind me of the good,

In everything.

And everything you have,

You give to share,
Even though at times,
I've little to bring.
You welcome me to your table,
When I am unable to sustain my soul,
My goal is to always be there for you,
Give you everything,
My all.
You call me clear,
You call me true,
Day by day,
I'm closer to you.
Any task that you may set,
Will be seen through to the end,

You are my Lord and Master,

My God and one true friend.

SLAIN

I've slain many demons over the years-

Faced myself in the mirrors,

Shed rivers for the fears.

None of those were easy,

Knowing each were never the last,

Casting doubt the depths of oceans-

Treading water on the past,

In fight of battle wide,

Inside a screaming flight of jackals,

Shackled in the storm,

With only the warmth of my heart for comfort,

To carry through the alarm.

One by one,

One fight at a time for each,

Reaching further forward in time,

And learning from what they teach.

Step by step,

With surety trodden,

None of the evil,

Will ever be forgotten.

So mirrors now,

They catch my stare,

I'm grateful now,

For the man standing there

DO NOT ADD BLEACH

Is there anything you can teach me,
About death and dying,
With persecutions away from truth,
To the fat lie now you're lying?
You try to tempt fate-
By telling me it's too late,
But perseverance shows its' proof;
The hooves of your horses have thundered
near,
And suddenly ground to a halt.
Faultlessly you have challenged me,
But I have shown no fear.
And now you are near you can see my
face,
But know that you cannot take my soul.
It has been your goal to challenge me,
And drag me back to hell,
I have stood at your gates relentlessly,
But now it's time to get well.
See if there is anything you can teach me,

About laying down so close to death,
Is you will never beat me,

Even beyond that very last breath

CRACKS (PART 1)

Do you ever feel like you're out of control?

Feeling the fear of what you just don't know?

Wishing you could step outside of your mind,

Just to find some relief of a kind?

Well release me.

Do you feel the need late at night to walk the street?

Scared of the thunder of your own heart-beat,

That only feeds the wonder of where heart and mind meet?

Take a seat and sit for a minute,

Meet your mind with mine I'm sure we could win it.

It could be real what we feel,

It should be!

The pain of the world on our shoulders,

Making us feel older with the strain,

We need to rein in that pain,

Put our heads together,

So tomorrow won't be the same.

It's draining on our hearts,

And it's draining on our minds,

The most upsetting thought of all-

I'm no longer shocked by what I find.

So don't be defeated as you sit there by my side,

It seems to be the product,

Of having a heart that's kind.

So rest your weary head a while,

Pile upon me all your woes,

I'll take the pain away from you…..

'till you feel the get up and go.

But you should know when you feel ready,

Thank-you for the sharing,

Now go take steps so steady.

Next time you feel like your head is gunna collide,

With a splittin' pain,

That makes you wanna run and hide,

Have the courage to find me,

And let your mind step outside,

And just for once-

Feel free.

THE UGLY SPECTRE

Ugly spectre you have raised your vicious head,

Dead I feel to the world,

With silence and darkness you have surrounded me,

But it's your truth I find absurd-

You want me to believe I am on my knees,

Never to dance once more-

Your score I know,

Yet I've still to hit the floor,

With dalliance I hold you in contempt,

Attempt me with all your will-

Still I will lie down,

and I will be here still,

You cannot control the magic in me.

Your dark cloak may surround me now,

But somehow I'll wait out your turn,

Put me to the test and do your best,

With your own iron I'll brandish and burn-

For though the end is far from sight,

Don't forget I've seen you before,

Forlorn I may appear just now,

But it's you that waged a war,

Your demons may dwell,

In every room in my mind,

And I may be locked in its' cellar,

But stellar am I and lest you forget-

In my house I'm the only dweller....

.....So open your dark curtains,

Let me see the shine of the moon,

Both of you are waning now,

And I will be home soon,

Learn your lesson and learn it well,

My home is in my heart-

And you are just a hotel,

I will always beat you,

In my own private hell.

SHELL

The rooms are empty,

They are just a shell.

It's all that remains,

Of my own private hell.

It use to hold demons,

On every floor,

But one by one-

I've shown them the door.

Exorcised by my own eyes,

Where I no longer listened,

To their twisted lies.

Mental records on every wall-

Twisted teachings,

Of times when I'd fall.

No failing light,

Bright in every room,

Now incandescent,

As I leave soon.

I'm just checking,

That there's nothing left behind,

And if I'd learned my lessons,

There's nothing to find.

So at last my mind,

Can finally rest-

It's forward to the future,

Now my mind has no test.

The rooms are all empty,

They are just a shell-

It's all that remains,

Of my own private hell.

OLD STORY

I wish I could tell a story,

In all its glory,

About the happy life I've had.

But what is perverse,

Is the dreaded curse,

As I'm afraid it's all rather sad.

Yes It makes me sad,

To think of all the wasted years-

Of their passing I'm rather glad.

But now my mettle is solid and sound,

And I know not no fears.

I'm chiseled and iron cast,

By lessons that last,

With both feet set on solid ground.

For the place that I've found,

Is happy safe and sweet,

For I'm happy when I look behind.

See I find I'd hit the bottom,

But none of it is forgotten,

As all of it is still quite loud.

I've trodden with heavy boots,

Upon my roots,

But now I wear them at leisure.

My past was a rocky road,

But now I'm walking the streets with pleasure.

See although I hit the bottom,

None of it is forgotten,

For I hold the past in a box,

Marked treasure,

THE MAGIC SWITCHES

The magic switches,

They're either off or they're on,

One minute you're weeping-

The next,

Singing a song,

From pounding rain in a storm,

To bright,

Sunny,

And warm,

From laughing with your best friends-

To wishing your life would come to its end,

From fertile land to barren soil-

One minute full strength,

Then weak from the toil.

From the joy of a new-born baby-

To the very spectre of death,

Those magic switches,

Can take your last breath:

Indeed,

Plant a seed,

The seed and that land,

Will give you a hand-

To lift you from the bottom,

And you will need those rain clouds,

To show you what was forgotten.

THE DARKNESS

ENTER THE DARK TUNNEL,

ENTER AT YOUR PERIL,

MAKE NO MISTAKE THERE'S NO-ONE TO TAKE,

YOUR'E THERE TO MEET THE DEVIL.

TO TORTURE YOU WILL GO,

NO LIGHT FOR YOU TO KNOW,

JUST DARKNESS DEEP AND TWISTED,

GONE INTO THE MISTS OF TIME,

WHERE ALL GOES SLOW-

AND MOTION CEASES TO A HALT,

AND BOLTS OF LIGHTNING SURROUND YOU,

AND FIRE TO WALK ON THE GROUND-

WHERE THE ONLY SOUND IS YOUR

SCREAMING,

AGAINST THE GLEAMING SCYTHE OF DEATH,

WHERE DEMONS AND THEIR PITCH-FORKS,

ARE THERE TO TAKE YOUR BREATH,

BUT DO NOT FLUSTER YOU WILL BE SOUND-

MUSTER YOURSELF YOU WILL BE FOUND,

SOLDIER ON TO THE SCYTHE AND FORKS,

THERE YOU WILL FIND THAT THEY CANNOT

WALK,

CARRY ON OVER, UP, THROUGH AND ABOVE,

SOMEWHERE THERE YOU WILL FIND THE DOVE,

FOLLOW HER 'TILL YOU SEE THE LIGHT.....

....AND BE TRULY GRATEFUL,

YOU GAVE IT ONE LAST FIGHT.

BACK IN THE SWIM

It's nice to be back in the swim,

From the deep,

To the surface.

And then to the shore: the hunger and it's
lasting,

That makes you reach out for more,

Dead to the was but still dying,

Sinking fast,

Then current lost,

And depth for past, destiny-the floor.

Yes destiny the bottom,

Ocean to swallow, and leave you forgotten.

But in the hearts last dying ember, of one last fire:

It's a glimmer of hope and trust that halts,

Then lifts us higher,

An institution of evolution:

Pain intact,

But nestling in comfort of emotive thought.

So then we lift,

To the surface then drift.....

.....in waves lost but in a retort:

A thin sliver of a swimmer,

And just a shade too close to a trance,

An undenied trance..

..glancing then fast:

But dancing.

Without doubt, a glimmer in a sea,

(A matter, alive in this universe-

A conscious self of me,

So swim I can,

And swim I will.

Out of this ocean and onto the beach)

Within my matter, undenied,

I have swum so fast,

And found the need to hide:

Yet I am not an empty shell,

Lying at the bottom of the sea:

I can see the shore, where I can be once more-

Back to the being they call me.

DREAMS

What would I write without a fight?

If events played in my mind,

Kept me awake through the night-

Rowing without a boat yet still keeping afloat,

Trying at best separating wrong from right,

Buoyant and correct fighting my intellect,

With the light of a lighthouse forever in sight.

Choppy waters all around,

In all that is found,

Yet rowing those oars with all my might-

Sirens ahead pulling me to rocks,

The creep at the back of my mind,

Coming forth in my head,

Strong will steering me,

Yet leaking with dread.

But the light of my lord illuminates,

From overhead.

Fighting storms in the calling,

Forever it seems,

Then soon to realise-

It's all in my dreams!

I MATTER

I don't wish to shatter the silence-

But I matter.

I don't wish to shout or use violence-

But I matter.

I won't be dismayed if you walk away-

But I matter.

I'd tell you of times if you'd listen to my lines-

And you'd shatter.

I'd tell you tales that would turn you pale-

And I matter.

You would be amazed at what has left me
unfazed-

And I matter.

I have distaste to your haste,

To dismiss me as waste-

For I matter.

So give me your ear and I'll make it clear-

That I matter.

You think I will shatter the silence,

And offer you violence-

That is the matter.

STRONGER THAN MY OWN DEMONS

You came to me in your rages

As you took my book of life

Then tried to rip out all its pages

You thought you could stand in front of me

In relentless shouts and screams

Enter my dreams to nightmare me deep inside-

So I just couldn't hide.

Wretched me

Wrecked me

Torn and twisted

But then you made the mistake-

You forced me to decide.

You'd took my feet

But I made a stand

You'd crushed my heart-

Yet I have my soul in my hands.

You tried to remove all glimmers of hope

When you dragged my head between your
gates

In your searing heat you forced me

To turn and run

Back toward true fate.

No I do not hate you

For that would be just in your flames

To be consumed

I'd rather run, love, and pray

Defy the weakness-

You wrongly presumed.

You thought I had no reason

To give you back the garrotte of your grip

That very last struggle of laboured breath

Was not for your conceit-

It was to buy back my own feet

Not in defeat.

In solid reliance

And in indomitable defiance

In the cracking of my own whip-

All four corners of my horses

In all my resources

Rear up now in sheer vehemence-

You're underfoot

Now it's you deep in the rut

See-

I'm stronger than my own demons.

www.ingramcontent.com/pod-product-compliance
Lightning Source LLC
Chambersburg PA
CBHW081931120726
47997CB00010B/3102